Arctic Lands

Published in the United States in 1982
by Gloucester Press
387 Park Avenue South
New York, NY 10016

Originated by David Cook and
Associates and produced by
The Archon Press Ltd
8 Butter Market
Ipswich

First Published in
Great Britain 1982 by
Hamish Hamilton Children's Books Ltd
Garden House, 57-59 Long Acre
London WC2E 9JZ

Printed in Great Britain by
W S Cowell Ltd
Butter Market, Ipswich

Certain illustrations originally published in
The Closer Look Series

U.S. ISBN: 531-03458-5
Library of Congress
Catalog Card No. 81-83205
ISBN: 0 241 10724 5

Arctic Lands

Consultant editor
Henry Pluckrose

Illustrated by
Maurice Wilson

small  world

Gloucester Press · New York · Toronto · 1982
Copyright © The Archon Press Ltd 1981

In the far north, the Arctic lands
surround the Arctic Ocean.
Another name for them is the tundra.
In winter, the days are short because the
North Pole faces away from the sun.

ARCTIC CALENDAR

January–February:
late winter, a dark
and cold time.

March–April:
early spring, but the
snow still falls.

May–July:
late spring, snow is
melting; days are long.

At midsummer, the sun does not set.
But it is only strong enough to warm
the top layer of earth.
About three feet (a meter) below the
surface, the ground stays frozen.

August–September:
summer, all the snow
and ice have gone.

October:
autumn, the first snow;
the lakes freeze.

November–December:
early winter, the land
is covered with snow.

Saxifrage

No trees grow on the tundra.
Since most of the soil remains frozen,
the roots could not grow and take in enough wc
But plants with shorter roots do live there.
They grow close to the ground where they are
protected from the strong Arctic winds.
Some plants, such as the Arctic poppy,
have hairs on their leaves and stems
to keep them warm.
The animals that live on the tundra rely
on these plants for food.

Reindeer moss is a
very important plant
on the tundra.
It is the main food
of caribou, lemmings
and other animals.

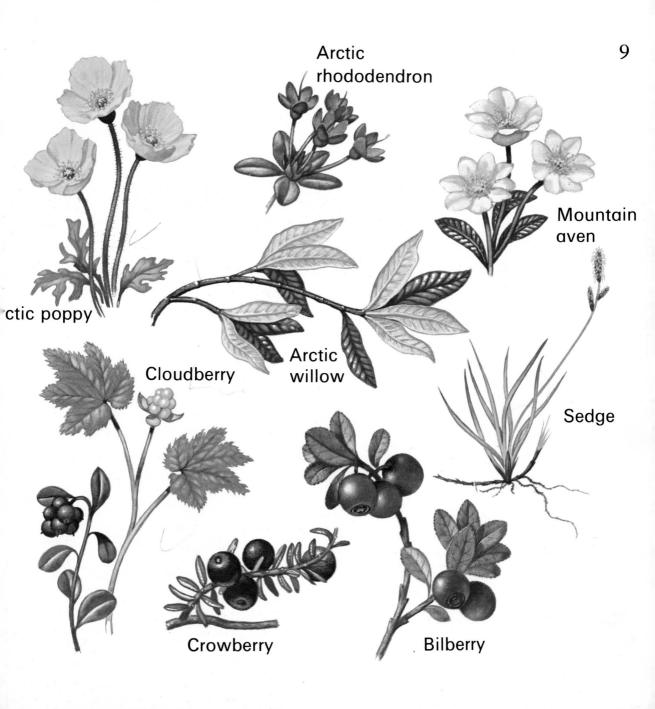

Arctic poppy

Arctic
rhododendron

Mountain
aven

Arctic
willow

Cloudberry

Sedge

Crowberry

Bilberry

Very few animals live on the tundra
throughout the year.
Those that do have adapted to the harsh
conditions there.
The Arctic fox turns white in winter
to make it difficult to see against
the snow.

Many tundra dwellers
grow white coats
for the winter.
This camouflages them
in the snow.

Ermine

Arctic
hare

Ptarmigan

Arctic
fox

All these animals live
on the tundra in both
summer and winter.

Gyrfalcon

Snowy owl

Arctic fox

Raven

Ermine

Redpoll

Meadow vole

Ptarmigan

Lemming

Arctic hare

Muskox

In spring, more than a hundred species
of birds arrive to nest on the tundra.
As they fly, they sing special songs
to attract their mates.

The picture shows some
of the birds which nest
on the tundra.

Barnacle goose

Brant goose

Arctic loon

Common loon

Knot

Lesser scaup

Sandhill crane

Red-breasted goose

King eider duck

Many have spent the winter in lands
far to the south.
Some come from as far away as Africa and
the Orient.

Blue snow goose

Whooper swan

Snow goose

Rock pipit

ewick's swan

Old-squaw duck

Northern phalarope

phalarope

Caribou are well-suited to the tundra. Their large hooves stop them from sinking into the snow in winter, or in the bogs in summer. Caribou are good swimmers.

Most tundra animals are visitors and only come for the summer.
These caribou spend the winter in the forests to the south of the tundra where it is warmer and more sheltered.
The caribou migrate north to the tundra in the spring.
Their calves are born in June.
They travel together in large herds.

Wolves follow the caribou and kill
any sick or injured animal that
strays from the herd.
Grizzly bears eat meat, but they
also like bulbs, roots and berries.
Because they are big and slow, they do not
hunt very well, but they will kill any
young or injured animal they find.
Wolverines, lynxes and foxes hunt
small animals, eggs and young birds.

Wolves attacking
a caribou

y bear

Wolverine

Lynx

Red fox

By midsummer, there are many different
animals on the tundra. Both residents
and visitors have finished breeding.
The ground is wet and boggy.
Water cannot escape through the ground,
because the earth is frozen below
the surface.

Tundra Animals

1. Ground squirrel
2. Sandhill crane
3. Whistling swans
4. Red fox
5. Eider duck
6. Red-breasted merganser
7. Old-squaw duck
8. Muskoxen
9. Caribou
10. Canada geese

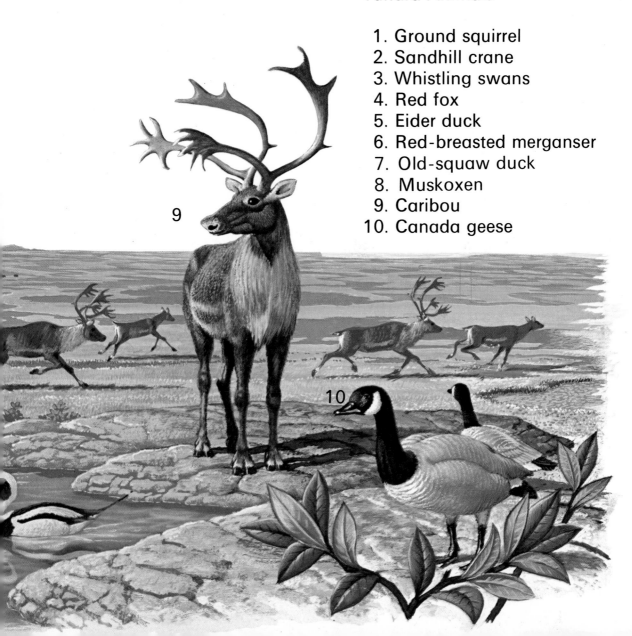

Lemmings are very small but very brave. They have been known to attack people who threaten them.

Lemmings are killed and eaten by many hunting animals.

Some years there are many more lemmings than others.

Lemmings breed very quickly. One mother can give birth to fifty babies a year.

The following year these babies produce their own babies.

Every fourth year there are so many lemmings that there is not enough food for them all.

Collared lemmings are the only rodents which turn white in winter.

Many of them become diseased and die.
Others set off in groups to look for
food. They may plunge into the sea
and drown, while trying to cross a large
body of water.
People used to believe that lemmings
drowned themselves on purpose.
When the number of lemmings has dropped
the lemmings that remain start to breed again.

The number of snowy
owl chicks a mother
can rear depends
on the number of
lemmings there are
for them to eat.

Canada geese are
joined by other birds
on their migration.

By August, some birds have left the tundra and the rest of the visitors are preparing to go.

By the end of September, they will have all gone.

To prepare for the winter, the animals that remain eat as much as possible. The food is turned to fat which will keep them warm.

Only the ground squirrel hibernates. It makes a nest deep in a bank and lines it with grass. It sleeps the whole winter through.

The nest of a ground squirrel.

By the end of October, the land is covered with snow. The larger animals live above ground; many small rodents live in tunnels beneath the snow.

Small animals such as voles and lemmings spend the whole winter underground.

Here they can keep warm. On the surface
they would quickly freeze to death.
Weasels search the tunnels for animals
to kill and eat.

It is always about
27° Fahrenheit
(−3° Centigrade) in
the tunnels below
the snow.

Other animals go to higher ground.
The wind blows so strongly that the
snow cannot settle and bury the frozen
plants the animals eat for food.

Caribou Eskimo

The tundra is the last great wilderness
left on earth.
But it seems certain it will not stay a
wilderness for long.
Oil and precious minerals have been
found there, and pipelines, mines and
roads have been built to help extract them.
The Eskimos who live there
have abandoned their traditional
way of life.
It may not be long before the tundra's
animals and plants disappear, too.

Index